THE METHODICAL MONSTER

THE METHODICAL MONSTER

FELIX NORTHWOOD

CONTENTS

Disclaimer

The content in this book is intended for informational and entertainment purposes only. While every effort has been made to ensure the accuracy of the information presented, the author and publisher make no representations or warranties of any kind, express or implied, about the completeness, accuracy, reliability, suitability, or availability with respect to the content of this book.

The views and opinions expressed in this book are those of the author and do not necessarily reflect the official policy or position of any individual, company, or organization mentioned. Any resemblance to actual persons, living or dead, or actual events is purely coincidental.

This book is not intended to defame, libel, or slander any person, company, or organization. All references to individuals, companies, products, and brands are for illustrative purposes only, and no affiliation with or endorsement by them is intended or implied.

The author and publisher disclaim any responsibility for any actions or outcomes resulting from the application of information contained in this book. Readers should seek professional advice or conduct their own research when making decisions based on the content provided.

CHAPTER 2

Introduction

"Here is your challenge. Show me a new standard of serial killer. Invent a new term that has nothing to do with how people usually think about it." This was the dare I received. So I looked into a man known as the "Methodical Monster". Not only is he said to be America's most elusive serial killer, some describe his crimes as "creative". But what's even crazier? On December 8, 2011, United States law enforcement arrested this man for credit card fraud. He had not committed a large enough crime for the FBI to pin him down, but what he didn't know was that some of the funds he funneled into his account as a result of a previous arrest, were stolen. Stolen from a bank that the FBI had interest in. A few months prior, in Anchorage, Alaska, an 18-year-old clerk named Samantha Koenig disappeared in the middle of her shift at a local coffee hut. The events that took place after her disappearance sent law enforcement on a years-long chase to track down her abductor, a quiet and unassuming contractor from Anchorage named Israel Keyes whose MO was suggests he was trained in the arts of hunting people, just as well as killing them.

CHAPTER 3

Chapter 1: The Early Life of Israel Keyes

The members of the tight-knit community of Stevensville, Vermont, spent time with their neighbors, and this was no different with the Keyes family, Glen the father, and Heidi the mother. They married young and had two children, a daughter born in 1972, known only by her assumed name here, Hillary, and a son, Israel, born in 1978. The quiet unassuming family kept busy on the weekends, splitting their time between family fun and small Jewish services and festivals through The Jewish People of Love and Peace. Passover was a favorite of Heidi's.

Israel's tumultuous early childhood would come to shape, if not warp, his future. According to Steve, Heidi put on airs to present the Keyes as an all-American family. But their marriage was severely flawed. Glen was a very intelligent man whose first love was education; he was an Annenberg scholar and newspaper editor. He wasn't overly ambitious but felt that he could always do what came his way better than anyone else. To escape his miserably unhappy marriage, he threw himself into his work and worked long and grueling hours as an investigative journalist. Glen was tough on Israel, and while always teaching him, Glen also consistently pushed his son to do better than he ever had. The father and son relationship ultimately suffered, especially once the separation came about and Glen began to exhibit physically abusive behavior towards the family. According to Israel, he fought with his father after seeing Glen hit Heidi and promised to attend his son's high school graduation.

Background and Family Dynamics

Israel Keyes grew up in a "happy, close family" with loving parents in a religious home. He was raised primarily in rural Washington State and then Maine after the age of 14. His father was a retired Marine and his mother was a homemaker. He had been homeschooled by his mother until leaving the Idaho basin. For a ten-year period, the Keyes family lived on Dutch Harbor in the Aleutian Islands, doing commercial fishing with their grandfather. Israel's sister later described the family as isolated and "raised in a fishbowl," as she and Israel wanted to be with the boy who sold candy, but they were not allowed to do so until they had received permission.

Three themes emerged as we examined the data - family dynamics that could have nurtured lethal behavior, outside-of-the-home influences that may have had an impact, and the way that Israel constructed his own narrative. In this section, we present the family dynamics that could have impacted Israel's mental well-being, and it is clear from the data that significant concerns were uncovered. According to Israel as well, the man in particular developed a nefarious reputation and that reputation of branding, kidnapping, sexually assaulting, and then killing the one or two daughters that were on every boat as captives fed into his thoughts. This, along with his strong religious background, could have influenced his dangerous behaviors later in life. Also, Israel's father has underscored the impression using a stick that Israel was exactly like him, and that his honesty was either unknown or just a mask that he used to deceive. Raised on the teachings of his father, Israel was taught that people were meant to be used by others; that God created some people for the purpose of being slaves. This opinion still appears to have shaped Keyes, as during his interview, he was careful to point out that it was not the force of law, but simply contempt for man's greed, that made it difficult for him not to kill.

Childhood Experiences

Keyes was born the second of ten children on January 7, 1978, and lived with his parents and siblings in a modest, modern home near the city of Colville, Washington for the first eight years of his life. Initially homeschooled through primary education, Keyes entered the public school system at age 8 and was placed in the fourth grade. Despite early assessment of a smashing success by his fourth-grade teacher, Keyes would experience isolation, racial bullying, and periods where he was suspended from school during later education.

In the seventh grade, Keyes wrote a list of 10 classmates that he wanted to kill and showed the bullet-riddled list to his friend, then threw it in a ditch. Referred to a psychologist, Keyes explained the distress he felt at his own inappropriate behavior. No further action was taken beyond brief intervention. In relation to this event, he stated to law enforcement that had he begun the stalking and killing, he would have targeted the "little bastards" who ads had helped him choose targets.

He became a father in his teens, but the relationship soured when the baby's mother, Tommy-Ruth, refused to perform a religious ritual on the child. Keyes was said to be "heartbroken" after the breakup. Group therapy reports from age 18 show Keyes firmly identifies as "on the outside looking in" and struggles with loneliness and rejection.

In an effort to overcome these feelings, he wrote a play in the form of a screenplay called Day of Reckoning. He acted in and directed the play for one showing at a local high school. At one point, he claimed to have co-authored a screenplay with an associate of the rapper Eminem but declined when the friend wanted to sell the screenplay. He was offered a role in B-movie Never Again but declined, perceiving it to be a step backwards. Instead, he wrote an unpublished 175,000-word novel called A Time to Hire. The novel blends first-person narrative and action from the novel and script, with the novel also including parts of the screenplay within the original narrative.

He is pro-white-heritage but identifies as a Satanist. He claims to have attended near-daily amateur boxing classes.

Formative Years and Development

Keyes' formative years set a foundation for character development that would foreshadow later emotions and behaviors. According to Lorelei, Keyes' mother, the highlight of his youth was when he competed in a rodeo at age 14. The Johnsons lived on a ten-acre ranch in their pre-urban Idaho hometown and bred both cattle and horses. Thus, Keyes would have been exposed to rodeos much of his life. Hastily, the theory that the rejection of a rodeo need sparked the series of killings was debunked by the FBI.

Israel Keyes was driven by a complex motivating system. It is important to understand these formative years and how character eventually developed and what motivated the man behind these crimes. Some FBI profilers believe that interpersonal violence and behavior are primarily driven by anger and hate. Israel Keyes did not have a rapid release of anger throughout his life; rather, he resembled a complex combination of revenge and financial gain with an unattached disposition. It is not probable that both parents were absent at all times. Parents need to attend to the family finances and to the other siblings, as is the case with two of Keyes' three sisters. Often, Keyes was at least age 14 or older by himself, with no one to look after him or keep him occupied. The immense freedom of Keyes' formative years lay critical, showing the amount of time he had available to lead his life unwatched, free to do anything without the need to report to anyone or to discuss hobbies with someone else.

CHAPTER 4

Chapter 2: The Crimes of Israel Keyes

"I like to think of it as a slide," Keyes confides in a federal investigator in the weeks following his arrest in March 2012. "I build my courage in stages. I'm two people basically. I have to face the dog first, then I need it to bark, then I have to knock it out. Then I can kill it." This chapter provides a behind-the-scenes look at Keyes's murders: his methodology, how he chose victims, what he did with them and their belongings, his aftercare to avoid detection, and the perfection with which he executed his crimes. Included are summaries of some of his known abduction kits, and also why he targeted Samantha Koenig and Bill and Lorraine Currier, his only known living victims. The chapter also details the investigation and discoveries that followed Keyes's arrest and death, unspooling the scale of his criminal past and offering clues to the possibility of many more victims.

The listener had questions. What about weapons? Keyes scorned knives, still used by amateurs with something to prove, leaving blood and murder evidence behind. For the same reason, with few exceptions, he avoided shooting and strangling. "You're leaving a lot of blood. You compromise too much. I strangled one," he said, "and

I'm not impressed." Yet when Keyes transported recovered weapons over state lines, he did so entirely on foot or by kayak, due to the peskiness of interconnected law enforcement databases, the official tracers of guns and other tools after sale—a different sort of forensic compromise, as far as he was concerned. So tools from a range of eras filled his trove: a Kimber .45 semiautomatic in Alaska, a Remington Model 7 rifle in New York's Adirondacks. Heads of hammers and mallets, hatchets small enough for a hiking pack—or for hacking off fingers and teeth. They just never got around to it.

Method of Operation

The method of operation, or modus operandi, of Israel Keyes is now relatively well-documented and suggests a criminal with a high degree of planning and behavior that reveals evidence of pre-meditation and researched selection of potential victims. Identifying possible personally preferred or highly likely hunting zones using certain victim characteristics, a quarter-mile distance and proportionate perimeter around state parks was then recommended to form a wide arc. Plastic ties, knives, rope, bonesaw, firearm, handgun, .22 rifle, and/or suppressor were recommended as concealed violation aids being possibly kept in a duffel bag. To assist others in identifying Keyes as a suspect, the serial number of his concealed evidence keys, F072 and F073, is provided.

One study done of federally incarcerated serial sexual homicide offenders showed that only 41% of them actually abducted their victims. Despite this, the vast majority of the publicly available fabricating narratives or speculative literature persists in describing a serial killer who will plant a location or a hunting ground, welcome friends or lovers into victims' lives or introduces the killer by arranging to meet his victims off the premises, prompt stalking, and/or plan the filed abduction of a certain person of a certain type. While this certainly is part of some serial killers' modality, it is not a global operational view of a serial killer classification. This research offers readers a view of Keyes's abduction methods that identify largely a reverse-engineering of a victim's ideal hunting zone based on a killer's operational patterns. Despite his complexity of approach, it is compelling for its possible ease of application given increased public access to online preparedness databases.

Abduction Techniques

In each of the investigations, the victim was addressed by their first name, suggesting that the assailant may have a false and friendly approach towards his victims. He stated that he used a ruse method to gain access to a domicile and abduct his victims during the hours of darkness or early morning while they were in their bed asleep. No suspects were developed or identified. Despite the differences in victimology, all of these cases were ruled as murder-suicides. Although unlikely, given the timeframe between the incidents, it is suspected that all of these victims were abducted from their homes. The tactic utilized in order to gain entry to these homes is also extremely similar to the confessions given by Keyes in regard to his tactics. Ireland spoke with investigative journalist Maureen Callahan and claims Keyes has a sexual disorder and fantasies that are not satiable.

Keyes stated that the abductions in Oswego and Lowell were opportunistic and stated that he abducted branch employees during the day and brought them to the secluded area. He did not do detailed surveillance on either of the locations prior to the abduction. In each investigation, Keyes indicated to the investigators that the sites were secluded and that he wanted the victims reported as missing and to be found by an unsuspecting person. Keyes did not take his kill kits or caches with him, he used the weapons and supplies that were available to him in the field. He stated the cashiers seemed ideal to abduct due to the late nights they worked, and how they were females without defense. The age range was appealing to him and he would purposefully pick new cashiers at the banks where he structured the abduction.

Known Victims

Known Victims That fit the problem with Keyes and that need to be remembered when discussing a serial killer so lethal and so cunning – he is a fiend that still clings to the darkness of uncertainties and long-lost secrets. The painfully few answers about Keyes will be presented here, but the many questions have no solutions. So we begin where he left off. This investigation into his crimes has been one without footprints. All that can be hoped for is that the sun will rise on Keyes and, in doing so, burn away ever-thickening layers of black. Lawmen already feel the heat, begging for immediate torches.

The unknown number of victims provided by Keyes could rise to a total of twelve when the conclusion gives the benefit of further consideration. Keyes was relatively forthcoming when it came to discussion about six of the people he abducted and killed. Indeed, the murderer's cooperation guaranteed there existed certainty for six of his crimes, a stark closeness the Justice Department of Anchorage is aware of. In time and as more information is made public, it is almost a certainty that Anchorage Law Enforcement will be forced to add names to the list of those Keyes has been credited with killing. Those six known Keyes victims are Robert Curley and Eklutna Annie, Bill and Lorraine Currier, Samantha Koenig, and Deborah Feldman. While words and recently released confessions have removed any remaining doubt tied to these murders, many details still elude the public and members of the press. All of our frustration at kept secrets, however, can do nothing to change the singular fact of the following nature: years passed before roughfooted lawmen managed to leave even these handful of welcomed tracks in the case of the fiendly unknown.

Investigation and Discovery

In 2012, FBI agents learned that Israel Keyes had been detained near Lufkin, Texas by the Jefferson County Sheriff's Office for a separate crime. They flew there while monitoring his interrogation and served Keyes a federal arrest warrant for the 18 U.S.C. § 875(c) violation.

In the week prior to the indictment, federal authorities began "digging information" from the known victims. This investigation unveiled the cryptic, non-cannibalistic habits necessary for Keyes to satisfy his curiosity. These inquiries suggested that Keyes was odd, didn't share his fancy meals, and seldom bragged about himself. To effectively control his urge to murder, he was rhythmically bearded, tattooed, and armed. He harbored a mobile prison, the features of which agents would discover two months later stashed in a shed, pausing absolute familiarity.

Here, Keyes revealed that he hadn't flown while scavenging many of the randomly selected women plucked from these venues. Yet, he flew and rented a car, now in Kona. The investigation into Keyes's travels, collect calls, and Kona's business burglaries provided leads to his lodging and the predatory, ritual kidnapping of the known victims. Rachel lived in a rented cinderblock cube where Keyes had engaged in murder nine months before in an expansive villa. Portions of conversations with other newcomers struggling alongside him in such the shared refuge convey the perverseness under which Keyes perpetrated these kidnappings and murders roughly two holidays past. It became evident now, some six weeks after Keyes's arrest, that there remained details beyond Rachel or Adams's recall that would furnish an accurate representation of Keyes's movements around the time of their respective kidnappings.

Chapter 3: The Investigation and Capture of Israel

He might not have a name, but law enforcement did know significantly more about the killer than when bodies started to surface. They knew he was white, in his mid-thirties to early forties, and that he had dark eyes, brown hair, and a lean build. Two suspects entered the task force's radar, but neither was a good fit. The first caught the group's attention after he was arrested for soliciting a prostitute, but he was leaving behind confessional notes laced with Christian symbols—an equally inaccurate trait. The second, a cellmate of the first suspect, had only been throwing off confessional notes in an attempt to lighten his sentence. "One hundred percent of the investigative leads had panned out in that case," Bill Rausch, an Army investigator assigned to the task force, said. The team's third attempt to identify the killer, however, worked thanks to a two-month effort between the local police and the FBI. After tracking down leads from the alibi-based suspects through Facebook, they eventually gathered enough information to link Keyes to Scratch.

The arrest was heavily coordinated between Alaska and the FBI in order to ensure their net encompassed three individuals but closed fast enough to prevent any career repercussions to Loren. Law enforcement arrested Keyes for both the Samantha Koenig abduction and her debit card use the next day. The SWAT team knocked on the front and back doors, catching Keyes off guard. The March 13, 2012, arrest took place in Katie's home. The crime scene specialists who entered the house on Spinner Court noticed that the house might have been rigged to capture contraband hidden in the home. They found a high-capacity drum for an automatic weapon, but Keyes only had a .22 on him. Yoshiko, the Keyes' ten-year-old daughter, happened to be in the house at the time of her father's arrest. She sat on the couch and watched as her father walked by. They intercepted her before taking Keyes outside. In an interview with Special Agent Jolene Goeden, Keyes confessed to the abduction and death of Koenig.

Initial Suspicions and Leads

When the FBI began investigating Israel Keyes as an alleged serial killer in 2012, they were surely aware of Keyes' cover-up skills, meticulousness, and understanding of investigative behavior. Law enforcement admitted it was as if he knew they were watching him. More than 17 victims were suspected during the early stages of the investigation between 2004 and March 2012 when Keyes was captured in Texas. When trying to understand his time frame, he suggested a range of two to twelve victims per year. Weekly trips in the United States were possible to travel with some ease.

The first murder that has been identified as Keyes' doing was scheduled to be a "murder kit" he placed at a remote trail near Tiedeman Slough Road in Oregon. The murder happened close to the beginning of 2001, in the same year he moved to Alaska. This was a pre-arranged attack but may have been earlier than the victim suggested. The trails around the Tiedeman Slough were a popular fishing area; the circumstances suggest he was recreational fishing. Similarly, he has indicated that his immediate vicinity will involve luring his victims. Keyes was known to prowl various locations (old barns, riverbanks, esker trails), independently of visiting the locations before committing a crime. Even though he has shown knowledge of the locations' existence, the specific choice by investigators may suggest he has not committed a crime there. The Kit was used to kill his first-known victims who drove to this location from Jantzen Beach with Keyes as their driver. Both victims died after a fast acceleration and striking the ground on their descent down a hill near the trail. Although the Kit was ready to go in the spring of 2001, he was no longer in a position to kill randomly. It is unknown how many Kits he placed in total. All in all, the killing was botched, and despite telling many of his confidants about the deaths he was directly responsible for, he did not seek further homicides until a series of unexplained killings would provide primary cover.

Interagency Cooperation

The capture of Israel Keyes was the result of extensive cooperation and coordination between multiple law enforcement agencies. Agencies involved in the investigation of Israel Keyes included dozens of local and state law enforcement. The Federal Bureau of Investigation took the lead agency role as well as providing the bulk of law enforcement resources specifically designated to investigating Keyes. This allowed for the federal government to provide resources to the smaller local and state departments that would have otherwise not been available. Along with the federal, state, and local law enforcement, there were also public agencies involved in the tangential aspects of the investigation. This included the United States Corps of Engineers as well as other federal park services.

The Army Corps of Engineers assisted in the case in multiple roles including management of the lakes where Israel Keyes dumped at least one body and the waterways where they think he cached his kill kits and murder kits with the intention of retrieving them at a later date. The FBI brought in the "BEST" Behavioral Analysis Unit to analyze Keyes' psychological profile and make determinations based on patterns and historical evidence about Keyes that turned out to be pivotal in pursuing him through relatively new forms of data collection that would otherwise have been dismissed as time-consuming, inconclusive, and with arguable privacy implications. All in all, there were over 20 agencies and non-profit organizations that, during the investigation, either directly affected or added value to the investigation as a whole.

Breakthroughs and Key Discoveries

The identification of Israel Keyes and the opening of the meticulous investigative file brought forth new strategies and tactics among those seeking to rewrite Keyes' profile as an elusive, hidden predator. The timely and fortunate discoveries and developments leading to these new and groundbreaking leads and investigative avenues put in motion the events that would ultimately result in Keyes' identification and arrest. The discovery of Keyes' name led, in short order, to investigations that produced at least six significant breakthroughs in less than fifty hours.

Firstly, Alaska officials quickly located Deborah Feldman, an assisting lab technician from the Best Western hotel chain who provided an answer facetiously labeled the Best Western bread and butter question. The investigation of Egland's computer, profoundly magnified by the contemporaneous tips from the public, produced two more breakthroughs. The accounts of Keyes' travels to and from Anchorage on behalf of his construction company, Keyes Construction, provided necessary background information to solve Feldman's bread and butter question. In addition, one of the recovered photos contained GPS information that accurately plotted the location of Israel Keyes, Samantha Koenig, and the Coffee Inn, where that photograph was taken. Within a few days, Alaska ASP investigators would discover all previous travels of the tough set of keys in Keyes' possession, including his recent entry from Canada.

A fourth breakthrough was generated by the release of Keyes' Anchorage International Airport security video by the Federal Bureau of Investigation. The video was forwarded throughout Alaska and quickly identified by those who knew Keyes and knew his proclivity for wearing his distinctive ball-cap. Keyes' name and role in the capture of the prolific serial killer "the Keyes stable hand" generated and triggered investigations into Keyes and Keyes Construction in three New England states he had traveled to in February 2012. The most significant of these investigations, however, was conducted in Ellsworth, Maine by Detective Dotty Small of the Hancock County Sheriff's Office and held the last of the six critical breakthroughs in the Keyes investigation in the short-term. A one-name, hybrid letter-number code found written on a traffic stop warning ticket issued to Keyes in the city in summer 2011 was the concrete match that positively identified investigator Keyes as America's most elusive serial killer.

CHAPTER 6

Chapter 4: Psychological Profiling of Israel Keyes

Psychopathy is a clinical diagnosis characterized by personality traits and behaviors that may seem extremely foreign to those of us who do not possess such personality dispositions. In fiction and in reality, psychopathy has long been linked with serial killing. Contrary to popular belief, not all serial killers are psychopaths, and vice versa. It was once believed by a majority of criminal justice and psychological professionals that psychopathy and similar personality disorders predicted extreme violent behaviors. While this may not be explicitly true, nations differ in the mechanisms by which violent behavior is predicted and therefore in the psychological tactics used to detect such behavior. The difference in these approaches is attributed to variation in cultural norms and values between nations. However, it is essential to also understand that while the exploration of psychopathy and serial killing may be of some relevance to professionals dealing with matters of forensic interest, these personality disorders are curiously rare when compared to the general population. Psychopathy and serial killing, when they do occur, are more commonly studied for the psychological questions they bring up and for the crimes' narrative interest, not solely for informative or criminal justice purposes.

We can, however, delineate some psychological traits that Keyes possessed that are relative and common amongst serial murderers. For Keyes, a repeated pattern of behavior was the systematic planning and organizing of each kidnapping operation. He would often invest a lot of time watching his assailants in a tireless search for a suitable victim and meticulously plan book flights, rental cars, and pay fines. This illustrates his organizational sophistication and his ability to continue planning and premeditating his crimes. Furthermore, it was of some significance in his handling of murder victims, the lack of forensic or physical evidence, and definitive link to his assaults and disappearances. Finally, the fact that the apparent injuries which the victims sustained as a result of the attacks were initially thought not to be suspicious raised considerable concern once again. His apparent ability to avoid detection does require the use of some cognitive skills, although these may not be in keeping with the rational thought patterns we regard as normal. In order to explore this, it was decided to conduct some psychological profiling of Israel Keyes.

Psychopathy and Serial Killing

Among those individuals who exhibit criminal behavior at the apex of human depravity are serial killers. Although some offenders may be impelled ethically toward such conduct by virtue of mental illness or traumatic brain injury, many consciously know that their actions are prohibited by the tenets of society.

Israel Keyes was clearly a man whose illegal actions were premeditated. All of the hallmarks of a serial criminal are present in his background: manipulation, criminal versatility, grandiosity, parasitic behavior, easy enchantment, pathological lying, and appearing to be 'superficially charming.' The extreme learnedness of this man demands an understanding of the stated psychological configuration in order to form any degree of comprehensive understanding. Psychopathy is well documented as one of the most common features of serial male criminals who murder. A ruthless mindset separates the abiding citizen from the true psychopath. Dr. Robert Hare defines the psychopath clinically in his well-known Psychopathy Checklist (PCL-R) as this: "a persistent pattern of irresponsible and antisocial behavior, decreased empathy and remorse, and bold, disinhibited, egotistical, egocentric traits." Any criminal individual like Israel Keyes will exhibit several or all of these traits. Keyes begins with the crime of bank theft (antisocial behavior), steals a case of computer files (no empathetic response toward a fellow human), and by doing so, an egotistical motive is apparent (renting a computer in order to steal sensitive data). Psychopathy is key to the reign of a methodical monster such as Israel Keyes. Contained within the primary description, a psychopath must unconscionably meet the two main criteria of this disorder, which are the complete lack of remorse and the complete lack of empathy.

Traits and Characteristics

The term "psychopath" has many characteristics associated with it, but to sum up, psychopaths are individuals with an antisocial personality disorder that predominantly lacks emotions such as love, empathy, anxiety, or fear. They are outstanding liars and manipulators, able to influence others by using the right words to sway people to their will. Very often, they seem to know all about you, solve your problems, and give excellent advice, creating a feeling of trust in their victims. This behavior to establish trust in their victims is characteristic of individuals with a "smooth," compulsive, or impulsive subtype of psychopathy in the US. However, the terms "psychopath" and "sociopath" are interchangeable and hold the same meaning. In the US, the term "sociopath" has a second meaning, which is used to describe individuals with the impulsive and aggressive subtype. On the other hand, when the purpose is to communicate with and frighten the victim, their family, or friends, serial killers usually show some clear distinctive behavior in communication compared to other psychopaths. In the past, one such example is Israel Keyes – a monster in the truest sense. To understand people like Keyes, we will now take an in-depth look into the characteristics of psychopaths and serial killers, along with their attributes.

Considering the history of serial killers, they have generally been diagnosed as psychopaths. According to Turner, "Show me a serial killer, and I'll show you a psychopath. It's virtually impossible to distinguish between the two." Furthermore, Hare & Babiak have listed strangeness, superficial charm, manipulation, cunning, pathological and compulsive lying, and absence of delusions or nervousness as some of the characteristics of psychopaths. Psychopaths play by the rules, but when the rules are not convenient for them, they tend to change them if possible because rules do not apply to them. In the present social context, Keyes had reluctantly found out that the "rules of confrontation" no longer play in his favor and found ways to have casts on one side and unconscious victims on the other side of the social battlefield. Thus, both serial killers and psychopaths are individuals who possess principles that matched Keyes to a great extent. He behaved as an individual with a strong will who can reconceive society, as opposed to prevailing social norms. It should be noted that a person can fit a number of criteria for being diagnosed with psychopathy but can never be perfectly categorized as a "pure" psychopath. Hence, such categorization cannot warrant the commission of criminal acts.

Motivations and Triggers

In discussions of motivation, it has been previously observed that extreme offenders are rarely the psychopathic "driven mass of ardent, compulsion-ridden fury," but instead usually act "out of cold detachment as sexual criminals, have a preference for necrophilic acts." These incredibly antisocial and damaging perpetrators often do not act in immediate response to a "sudden 'trigger'... experienced as pleasure," but instead develop desires for inflicting pain and crossing moral boundaries over a protracted period of time. These murderers typically act out after a "series of 'encounters' with a variety of sexual excitation situations that expedite a wider range of permissible and pleasurable experiences, although with little or no immediate 'schema pleasure.'"

These deviant sexual motivations and triggers build upon one another, with the desire to commit increasingly taboo behavior developing after each experience. These are in line with the observations made by Israel Keyes' friend that, "Into the mind through the eyes," describing a calculative, methodical psychopathy that Keyes himself would empathize with. Keyes' own confession in a police interview also reinforces this view: He himself concurred with his friend's formulation of fantasies as animated with a "sensation" that made him "feel alive." Statements from Keyes' interviews also give insight into the motivations behind his torturing of his victim. He responded to a description of his victim's last moments by saying that, "Now that's a feeling." In particular, he showed a marked preference for "digging into what makes someone tick" and for getting people to "open up to him"—in part because the most boring people were also the most predictable, unlike himself. "I'm two different people basically... both have the same concept of what is with the world around them, but just a different view," he would later describe his inner conflict.

CHAPTER 7

Chapter 5: Impact and Legacy of Israel Keyes

The abhorrent actions Israel Keyes carried out throughout 2011 and 2012 disturbed the American public deeply. This chapter is intended to explore the impact and legacy Keyes had after his heinous acts were revealed to the public and press. Channel 2's "Methodical Monster: Unfolding the Mind of Serial Killer Israel Keyes" revealed his entire life story, in and out of prison. I made appearances in all five episodes and was delighted when I was told it aired as an anniversary special of sorts on December 1, 2018, and remained on Hulu and other streaming channels until late 2019.

Israel Keyes has, in some ways, been forgotten by the general public, which is a crying shame. However, in law enforcement and forensic fields, Keyes has caused major policy and procedure changes. With the expert work of "Jay," working an inside job, and myself, many of the hundreds of law enforcers Israel Keyes spoke with and confessed to in Anchorage, Alaska, were made aware. Most law enforcement personnel were instructed to keep the matter quiet among their agencies, and only a very small contingent was allowed to be awakened between 3 A.M. and 5 A.M. to listen to a live streaming of the arraignment out of Anchorage for Keyes' murders of Bill and Lorraine Currier. Authorities on the scene of the investigation, and a few federal and local representatives, stayed on the scene during the arraignment and associated festivities.

Media Coverage and Public Perception

It was only "weird" that he had committed these murders. If you have a "normal life", of course you try to cover up what you do. You know it's not a totally "normal" thing. Turning to the micro-level analysis of murderer studies, the following sections consider if the public understandings that Israel Keyes cannot be a serial killer are framing mechanisms similarly to "excuses", presenting explanations that render some of Keyes' traits, actions and relationships with others understandable within a framework of normality.

The crimes of Israel Keyes ruminated through the Internet and traditional news articles, stringing together details of how Keyes came into contact with individuals through "tattoo trends", fascinated with "missing people", especially children. Israel Keyes crimes caught the public attention, but caused little panic and did not enter into the public consciousness as had the cases of Zodiac, Jack the Ripper and "BTK". Blog sites often talked of the irony of Keyes father being a Christian pastor and of his revelations that during Bible studies and Sunday services he wished God would help him, claiming that "I fought on behalf of my people, and placed judgement on others who chose to do evil." either consciously or unconsciously projecting the knowledge of the nature of his acts and desires. America's strongest frame of an ordinary, if particularly bizarre, man incapable of the extreme and intimate crimes he was accused of committing did not alter with the boundaries of race. The Minneapolis media had in their reports stressed that Israel Keyes learnt to think like a criminal from growing up on the wrong side of

Minnesota's largest prison and grew into an embodiment of prison friendships.

Lessons Learned and Policy Changes

The case of Israel Keyes has left its mark on many people and should serve as a sobering reminder of the kind of dangers we are dealing with. The investigation revealed a man that adapted to circumstances, changed his methods of operation, and evolved as an offender. The actions of Keyes - maintenance free and Keyes-specific property to store his murder kits in an area where friend-of-a-friend rules and old-boys networks are still the norm and access to storage is difficult - show the adaptive levels Keyes went to to stay under the radar. For years, this man hid in plain sight, thrilled by the power he felt and the suffering of others. The sad reality is one reason that Keyes was able to do this for as long as he did was because the rules and regulations of law enforcement and the criminal justice system are not equipped to deal with someone like Keyes. But the actions of Keyes have prompted a lot of changes.

Not only has Israel Keyes himself been a catalyst for the kind of adaptive changes that are put in place within the aftermath of a case, but the investigation itself has also had a significant effect on the way these lessons are learned. Since his arrest, jurisdictions are reporting that this is leading directly to new protocols being put in place and paradigms are being directed by the above issues. The challenges and lessons learned from the investigation are also the theme of Special Emphasis Report 13-31.

CHAPTER 8

Conclusion and Reflections

To investigate Israel Keyes' case attempts to uncover the methodology and interaction of behaviors that allowed for more than a decade of unsoiled identity. His successful evasion from an informant-purgatory travels beyond the examination of his psyche and into the systems of criminality, convicting justice system, and cultural images of the serial killer. This makes the elucidation of his 'monsterdom'-by-numbers to be the most concerning discovery of all.

Throughout this book, I have reflected on the systemic affordances of Keyes' plans and actions. The constructed mythology of the serial killer fixates on key features in a public "pillow tabloids" and "crime stories" that pander to the rubber-necking need for gore in the western imagination. More problematically, these images operate as a mask that even faced with the reality of a Keyes, still exist as a monolithic model of monsterdom. Thus, framing him as the most successful of serial killers is not surprising. In this image-saturated saturation, it was profoundly easy for Keyes to access, control, and exit as quickly as he did. His laconic narratives reflect his deep understanding of the mythology by-the-numbers, and enabled him to slip through federally networked databases and local law enforcement agencies. In this way, then, Keyes' methodology is not just his method or means to which he killed and hid bodies, but also a combination of systemic criminality, meaning, and visual saturation. The weight of these factors is presented in table 1, in the form of a word cloud which visually depicts the intersections of Keyes' narratives, locations, and bodies.

CHAPTER 9

References

Keyes, J., & MacLeod, D. (2012). Why an Alaskan Traveler is Now Considered the Most Meticulous Serial Killer in the United States. People Magazine.

Turner, L. (2013). Blood Lust: Portrait of a Serial Sex Killer. Amazon Digital Services.

McSkimming, N. (2021). Monster: Murder, Hate, and Madness. Amazon Digital Services.

Toth, M. (2021). Birth of a Monster. The True Crimes Book Club

Bennett, M. M. (2013). I've Been Watching You: Inside the Minds of Serial Killers. Amazon Digital Services.

Bosma, C. A., & Kennedy, K. (1989). How to Uncover Your Past Lives. Snowy River Press.

Davis, K. (1971). And the Sea Will Tell. Amazon Digital Services.

Extreme Stalkers Motivated by Rejected Love. (1999, May 25). New Sunday Times (Kuala Lumpur), p.14.